NICOTEXT

PARKLIFE

What is a park?

Definition from a dictionary:
"A park is a bounded area of land, usually in its natural or semi-natural (landscaped) state and set aside for some purpose, usually to do with recreation."

Definition from a normal person:
"A green place filled with flowers and trees where you hang out, have fun and relax."

Games/Relax

■ The game of horseshoes

Divide players into two teams and give each team two horseshoes. Flip a coin to determine who will start. Make sure that the stake is 25 to 40 feet away from where the players will pitch the horseshoes.

The first player throws both horseshoes towards the stake. Then, the first player from the opposing team will also throw both horseshoes. To score, give 1 point for each horseshoe within 6 inches of the stake, 2 points for a horseshoe touching the stake, and 3 points for any horseshoe that is encircling the stake.

After adding the scores, the next two players will throw their horseshoes from the opposite end of the "court." Add their scores to the first scores and have team members alternate pitching the horseshoes from one end of the "court" to the other. The first team to accumulate 40 points wins the game!

■ Limbo

Designate one or two people to be in charge of holding a limbo stick. Start the music and each participant is to walk under the stick. Make sure to start with the stick high enough that everyone can clear it easily. Once everyone has passed under the stick, the stick holders need to lower it gradually.

With the stick lowered, participants must bend backwards to clear it, and they are not allowed to squat or stoop. Anyone who cannot clear the stick is eliminated from the game. Keep lowering the stick till there's only one person left.

■ Frisbee golf

Set up 7 sticks or goals of some kind. Throw the frisbee to each goal, just like golfing. The least shots wins!

■ Kubb

Kubb is a game where the object is to knock over wooden blocks by throwing other wooden blocks at them, and finally to knock out the "King" standing in the middle.

Start by dividing players into two teams. Each team gets six sticks. The first team throws the six sticks, from their baseline, at their opponent's lined-up kubbs. Throws must be under-handed, and the sticks must spin end over end!

Kubbs that are successfully knocked down are then thrown by the first team onto the second team's half of the pitch, and stood on end.

The game then changes hands, and the second team throws the sticks at the first teams' kubbs, but must first knock down any standing field kubbs. Again, kubbs that are knocked down are thrown back over onto the opposite half of the field and stood on end.

If either team leaves field kubbs standing, the kubb closest to the king now represents that side's baseline, and throwers may step up to that line to throw at their opponent's kubbs.

Play continues in this fashion until a team is able to knock down all kubbs on one side, from both the field and the baseline. If that team still has sticks left to throw, they may make one attempt at knocking over the king. If a thrower successfully topples the king, they have won the game.

■ Bocce

Divide players into two teams of one, two or four players each. Each team gets four balls.

Have a player from the first team stand behind the foul line and throw the small ball, or "pallina," toward the opposite end of the playing surface. Let the player then throw one of the larger balls, or "boccia," trying to get it as close to the pallina as possible without touching it.

Have players from the second team take turns throwing their balls until one of the balls stops closer to the pallina than the starting player's ball. If they fail to do so, the starting team tries to outdo its first attempt. Let the starting players take their second turn if the opposing team gets closer to the pallina than the starting team without using all of their balls.

Continue until all eight balls have been thrown. The team with the closest ball gets one point for each of its balls that are closer to the pallina than the other team's closest ball. (Remember: if the two teams' closest balls are an equal distance from the pallina, no points are awarded).

End the frame after all eight balls have been thrown and appropriate points have been awarded. The scoring team begins the next frame. If no team previously scored, the team that threw the pallina last begins the next frame. Play as many frames as needed until one team has a total score of 16 points.

■ **Relax in the park**

- Sunbathing
- Go for a long walk
- Read a book
- Meditate
- Go fishing
- Take a nap

Words of advice:

Turn off your cell phone, so it won't disturb you.

Load your Ipod with aniti stress tunes.

Tip!

Some parks have designated quiet zones. If you're in Central Park for instance, visit Strawberry Fields, Sheep Meadow, East Green, Conservatory Garden, Shakespeare Garden, and Turtle Pond. Many parks have quiet zones.

Observe! These quiet zones do not allow running, rollerblading, bike riding or explosions of any kind.

No organized, active recreation or sports are allowed and you have to keep your dog in a leash. A good place to eat an entire cake by yourself in other words.

■ Meditation through deep breathing

"Take a deep breath" is common advice to soothe people who are stressed or upset. And fact is, deep breaths, or so called deep breathing, is the essential part of meditation. You see, we forget to breath properly when we're feeling stressed, and start breathing only in our chests, using short, shallow breaths.

This is how you meditate:

When you're meditating through deep breathing, you breath in through your nose and then you let the air hiss out through your mouth. The exhalation is slow, your thorax and your stomach are raised when you inhale and go down when you exhale. You instantly become more serene when you're using deep breathing. Deep breathing brings oxygen to your brain, and nerves and muscles are relaxed.

■ Meditation through breathing

Meditation through breathing has the same function as deep breathing; to slow your breathing down.

This is how you do it:

Check your breathing by counting in your head between breaths. Start with counting to one between every breath, and then gradually increase it to eight. This calms your breathing down and gives it a lower pace.

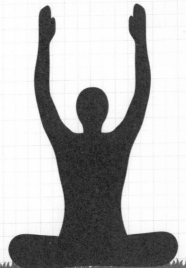

■ Classical meditation

The classical meditation is simple and based on you sitting comfortably on a blanket or parkbench. Keep your eyes closed while doing this exercise.

This is how you do it:

Sit in a bench and make yourself comfortable, your back should be in good contact to the back support. Your feet rest firmly against the ground and you can let your hands rest in your lap. Close your eyes and feel your muscles relax and breathe slowly through your nose. You can also repeat a word to yourself if you want. By doing that, your attention is focused towards only one thing, which keeps your "usual" thoughts away for a while. This provides your body and head with some rest.

Have a fun day in the park with your kids!

■ Infants and toddlers (0-4 years old)

Suggestions of activities:

- Feed the ducks
- Go for a nature walk
- Visit the zoo
- Have a picnic
- Visit the playground
- Take a walk in the stroller
- Take a swim in the zero-depth play pool
- Go treasure hunting
- Do face painting

The "don't forget"-list

- Diapers and wipes
- Changing pad
- Stroller
- Rain cover for the stroller
- Bottles, nipples, bottle caps
- Sippy cup
- Baby food, spoons, bowl with lid
- Bottled water
- Snacks
- First Aid
- Medical bag
- Sunhat

■ The park with older children (4-11 years old)

Suggestions of activities:

- Go hiking
- Try horseback riding
- Swim in the pool
- Try skateboarding
- Make a bike safari
- Visit the zoo
- Gaze at stars at night
- Play soccer
- Play hide and seek
- Have a picnic
- Go on a boat
- Go fishing

The "don't forget"-list

- Bottles of water
- Sunscreen
- Rain coat
- First Aid
- Extra clothes
- Blankets
- Sunglasses
- Snacks
- Insect repellant
- Moleskin for blisters, elastic tape, scissor

■ Park games for kids

Balloon Toss

What you need: Water balloons

Have the kids pair up into groups of two and stand opposite each other. Each pair should be equal distance apart. Give each pair a water balloon and have them toss it to each other. After each toss, everyone takes one step back. Keep tossing and stepping! The game continues until only one team is left with an intact water balloon.

Jump Rope Race

What you need: 3 jump ropes

Divide the kids into equal teams and line them up in their teams behind a starting point. Lay one jump rope in the grass at the other end of the yard. Have one kid from each team jump rope across the grass to the finish line and back. When they reach the starting point, the next player goes and so forth. The team that finishes first wins.

■ Park games for kids

Octopus Tag Game

What you need: Nothing

Set up a rectangular "ocean" in the grass. All the players but one, the Queen Octopus (or King), line up at one end. The Queen (or King) stands in the middle and cries out:

"I am the Octopus, queen (king) of all motion. Let's see if you can cross my ocean."

The Fish then try to run or sneak across the ocean as the Octopus tries to tag them. If tagged, they become Seaweed. Keeping one foot planted, Seaweed try to reach out and tag the Fish running by, thus turning those players into Seaweed as well. Once the Fish reach the other side, the Octopus and Seaweed say the chant and the crossing contest starts again. The game continues until all the Fish become Seaweed. The last Fish tagged becomes the new Octopus!

■ Park games for kids

Duck Duck Goose

What you need: Nothing

Have the kids sit in a circle facing one another and choose one kid to be "it". Their duty is to walk around the outside of the circle, tapping each child's head – calling out "duck" or "goose." "Ducks" stay put, but a "goose" must get up and chase the "it" person around the circle. It is the goal of the "goose" to tap the "it" person before they are able to sit in the spot left behind by the newly chosen "goose."

If the "goose" catches the "it" person, then "it" must sit in the middle of the circle and the "goose" becomes "it." As the game continues, the person in the middle is not allowed to leave their center position until another player is tagged and they are replaced.

I Spy

What you need: Nothing

One person chooses an object they see outside and gives one clue until someone guesses what they have chosen. The first person to play might say, "I spy something with my little eye and the color is green" or "I spy something with my little eye and it is shaped like a circle." The person who guesses right gets to choose his or her own object to give a clue for in the next round.

Important!

Remember to always keep your child supervised!

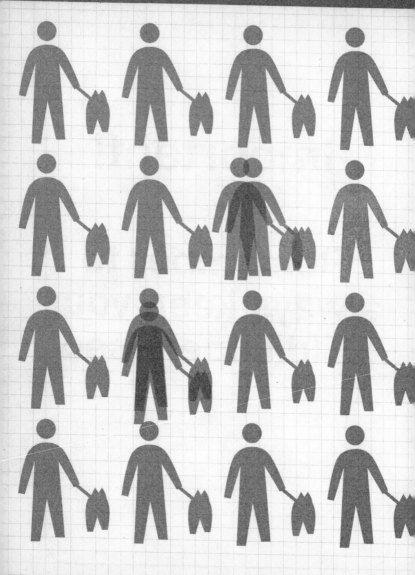

With your dog in the park

■ With your dog in the park

Suggestions of activities:

- Throw a frisbee
- Toss a ball
- Visit the dog park
- Take a long walk in the woods

- Take a jog with your dog, a so called Dogjog!

Dog Park Rules:

Any bodily injury and/or property damage caused by your dog, is your responsibility.

You must keep your dog supervised at all times.

You have to keep your dog in a leash on appointed places.

Only healthy dogs should visit dog parks.

Remember to always scoop your poop!

Food/Drink

■ Picnic

What to pack for a picnic:

- Tablecloth or blanket to sit on
- Forks, spoons and knives
- Cups
- Napkins or a roll of paper towels
- Bug spray
- Salt and pepper
- Aluminum foil and containers for leftover food
- Can opener
- Ice packs
- Corkscrew
- Umbrella
- Sunscreen
- Garbage bags

■ Suggestions for different kinds of picnics

Vegetarian picnic

Halloumi cheese sandwich
Summer green bean salad
Grilled beany zucchini
Potato rolls
Spanish style tortillas with spinach
Cajun potato salad
Melon
Mango iced tea
Bean and cheese dip
Bruschetta with goat cheese and pesto

Family picnic

Chicken wraps
Steak sandwich
Grilled Pizza with tomato and cheese
Chicken sandwich
Hamburger and hot dog rolls
Banana boats
Marinated pork
Blueberry lemonade

Mezze picnic

Couscous salad
Hummus with pita and vegetables
Spicy sausages
Artichoke salad
Marinated lamb kabobs

Mexican picnic

Beef tortilla
Guacamole
Mexican corn and black bean salad
Sangria

Romantic picnic

Clams
Oysters
Caviar
Chocolate
Strawberries
Grapes
Champagne

■ Picnic drinks - with alcohol

Sangria

1 part soft red wine
1 part orange juice
1 part lemonade

Rum Punch

2 parts soda
1 part dark rum
Frozen orange-pineapple juice concentrate
1 cup coconut rum

Champagne Punch

1 bottle Sauterne Wine
4 bottles of champagne
2 bottles of ginger ale
Lime sherbet
Ice cubes

■ Picnic drinks - without alcohol

Party Punch

1 can frozen lemonade
1 can well chilled Hawaiian Punch
2 bottles well chilled ginger ale
Frozen, sliced strawberries

Malibu Punch

1 bottle orange Juice
1 bottle pineapple Juice
1 bottle peach Juice
1 bottle grape Juice (Sparkling)
1 can cherries

Fruit Punch

1 can frozen orange juice
1 can frozen lemonade
1 can pineapple juice
2 bottles ginger ale
1 pkg frozen strawberries

■ How to keep the picnic cold

Summer is the perfect time to have a picnic. The only problem is it's hard to keep picnic foods cold. Here are some tips...

• Prepare your picnic food the night before the event. This way, all foods will be thoroughly chilled.

• Put frozen bottles of water in your picnic bag/cooler! This will keep your picnic foods cold for hours.

• Put the picnic bag/ cooler in the shade.

• Instead of setting out all of your picnic foods, keep the cold items in the cooler. Make sure you keep the lid on.

• Don't leave the picnic food out on the picnic table. Put leftovers back in the cooler as soon as you're finished eating.

■ BBQ for beginners

Some advice for the barbeque picnic!

• Make a nice pile of charcoal. Start the fire 45 minutes before it's time to start the actual barbequing.

• If the fire isn't hot enough; add additional charcoal. If things are too hot, raise the meat on charcoal. You can also close the air intake holes to lessen the fire.

• Lay the meat down on the grill, use a spatula or a fork to turn the meat.

• You will know when the food is done by using a bi-therm instant read thermometer. Insert the thermometer for 10 to 15 seconds, then determine the meat's internal temperature.

• Remember: Barbecuing is usually only allowed in designated areas, and no barbecuing is allowed under trees!

■ My own picnic recipes

Write down your favorite recipes

-

-

-

-

-

-

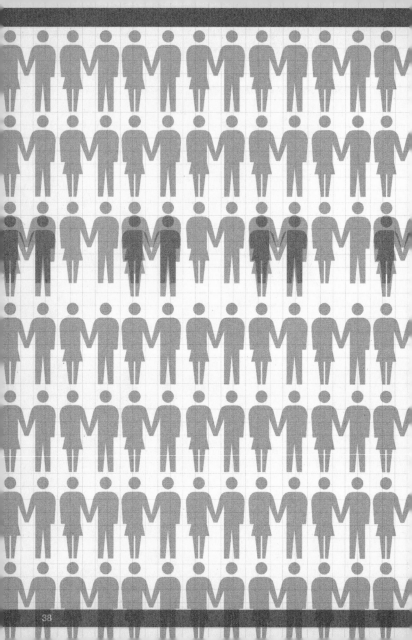

Flirting/Hanging out

■ Great places in the park to flirt

Dog park
The dog park is the perfect place for flirting. Don't have a dog? Borrow one from a friend who's "out of town" for a few days. A cute puppy will work as a babe magnet.

Park bench
Flirt with the person sitting next to you.

The running track
Put on your best training outfit and start flirting at the running track! Maybe you can ask him/her: "Hi... would you mind showing me how to do that stretching exercise?"

The "lunch area"
Many office workers are out for lunch in the park, and who wouldn't want some flirting for lunch?

Tourist attractions
Most parks have some form of tourist attractions. Flirt with a tourist! Offer to be his/her guide during their stay in the city.

■ How to flirt

1. Make eye contact

2. Use an opening line

3. Keep up the flirting

4. Get his/her number!

■ Great pick up-lines for the park

- Is it hot today or is it just you?

- Do you believe in love at first sight or should I walk past again?

- Excuse me, do you have Band-aid? I skinned my knee when I fell for you.

- You're so hot that you make the sun jealous.

- Is that the sun coming up... or is that just you lighting up my world?

- Hi

■ Find new friends

- Race someone at the running track.

- Ask if someone wants to go rowing with you.

- Get a group of friends together and challenge another group for a game of soccer in the park.

- Start a conversation with someone on a park bench.

■ Hanging Out

In case you need something to say, these are things to discuss:

- Travel
- Movies
- TV
- Books
- Sex
- Relationships
- Gossip
- Celebrity spottings
- Squirrels
- The color red
- Deep sea fishing
- Chestnuts
- Dreamjobs
- Aliens
- Laura Palmer
- Muffins
- Roadtrips
- Parties gone wrong

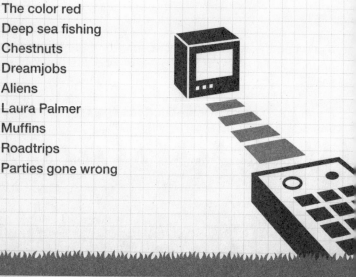

■ Truth or dare

Rules:
Spin a bottle and pick truth or dare. When you've answered a truth or performed a dare, the next player continues. Make up your own questions or use the ones below!

Dare

Allow the other participants of the game to use your cell phone for sending a text message to any person in your address book.

Make fart-sounds with your mouth, as loud as you can.

Pretend like you don't know the participant opposite you and try to pick him/her up.

Truth

If you had the chance to ask absolutely anything and was guaranteed an honest answer, who, and what, would you ask?

If you could make a "one-hour sex-change", what would you do?

What's the bitchiest thing you've ever done?

■ Tear-out-notes

Some days you just don't feel like talking to anyone, but that sucks because that could be the day you meet your new friend or loved one. The solution is a totally new and high tech devide that will cut through silence like a hot knife through butter. We call it: **a Note!**

Just write down your info, tear it out and hand it over!

I like you.

_____
_____
_____

This is me

....

Want to go birdwatching with me?

This is me

....
....
....

You are cute, call me.

....
....
....

This is me

....

Meet me by the

....

.... at ....

....

This is me

....

....

....

You're so hot that you make the sun jealous.

This is me

....

I want to take you out on a picnic.

Meet me at..............

on..............

This is me

Sweat in the park - sports and workout

■ Sports

Suggestions of sports fitting for the park:

- Baseball and Softball
- Volleyball
- Basketball
- Bicycle Riding
- Boating
- Running/ jogging
- Yoga
- Rock Climbing
- Football
- Frisbee and Frisbee golf
- Kayak
- Handball
- Horseback Riding
- In-line/ roller skating
- Swimming
- Tennis
- Walking
- Horseback riding
- Skate boarding

■ The "don't forget"-list for sports

- Bottles of water

- Sunscreen

- Insect repellant

- Moleskin for blisters, elastic tape, scissor

- Sunglasses

- Possible sporting equipment

■ Work out on a park bench

Many gym exercises can be easily executed on a park bench, they just need to be slightly modified. Here are five exercises for you to do on a park bench!

Thighs

1. Stand facing a park bench.
2. Lift your right foot onto the seat of the bench, so that your thigh and calf form a right (90°) angle.
3. Step onto the bench, bringing your left leg onto the seat.
4. Lower your left leg and place your foot on the ground.
5. Lower your right leg, so that you're standing with both feet on the ground.

Abs

Sit at one end of the bench. Your legs should form a parallel line with the length of the bench. Hold onto it with both hands on either side of your buttocks. Lift your legs towards your torso into a squatting position. Be careful; your feet shouldn't touch the seat of the bench. Stretch your legs out in front of you, leaning slightly backwards. You'll feel tension in your abs. Hold yourself firmly with your arms. Bring your legs back up towards you and start over.

■ Work out on a park bench

Triceps

Position yourself with your back to the seat of the bench. Place the palms of your hands on the edge of the seat. Keep your elbows slightly bent; your body should form a chair-like position, with your thighs and calves at a right angle and your arms straight. Then, bend your elbows and lower your buttocks to the ground. Straighten your elbows and lift your butt back to the initial position. Do two sets of 15 lifts, resting 30 seconds between each.

Biceps

For a beginners' level of difficulty, place yourself in the starting position for a normal push-up, but with your hands on the back of the bench, rather then on the ground. Bend your elbows and start doing push-ups.

Glutes

This exercise works your glutes (that's your butt), your obliques (sides of your abs), and your inner and outer thigh muscles. Position yourself behind the bench, grabbing hold of its back with both hands. Lift your left leg up sideways, until it forms a parallel line with the length of the bench. Lower your leg to the ground and bring it back up again.

■ Work out with a tree

Biceps

1) Find a good low tree with sturdy branches.

2) Hold on to the tree branch with both hands.

3) Bend your arms, pull your torso upwards so that your full body weight is supported by your arms.

4) Lower your body back down.

■ Interval on hill/mountain

1) Pick a hill/mountain.

2) Climb or sprint for 60-120 seconds.

3) Rest for 90-120 seconds.

4) Repeat 6-8 times.

■ Try step-up on a rock

1) Find a rock that's about 50 cm/20 inches high.
2) Step up.
2) Step down.
3) Keep your back straight and your head up,
repeat 10 times.

Don't forget to stretch!

■ Power walking - how to walk faster

Power walking is walking at a speed at the upper end of the natural range for the walking gait. Power walking is equally efficient as jogging. Here are some tips on how to walk faster!

1. Use good posture. Walk tall, and look forward, Your chin should be level and your head up.

2. Keep your chest raised, and shoulders relaxed.

3. Bend your arms in slightly less than a 90 degree angle. Cup your hands gently. Swing arms front to back. Do not swing elbows higher than your breast bone. If you swing your arms faster, your feet will follow!

4. Tighten your abs and buttocks. Flatten your back and tilt your pelvis slightly forward.

5. Pretend you are walking along a straight line. To go faster – take smaller, faster steps.

6. Push off with your toes and land on your heel, rolling through the step and pushing off with your toes.

7. Breath deep and rhythmic.

■ Outdoor yoga

Mountain Pose

1. Come to stand with the big toes touching.
2. Lift up all your toes and let them fan out, then drop them down creating a wide solid base. You can separate your heels slightly if your ankles are coming together uncomfortably.
3. Bring your weight evenly onto all four corners of both feet.
4. Let the feet and the calves root down into the floor.
5. Engage the quadriceps and draw them upwards, causing your knee caps to rise.
6. Rotate both thighs inwards creating a widening of the sit bones and tuck your tailbone in between the sit bones.

■ Outdoor yoga

The Tree

1. Come to stand in Mountain pose.
2. Feel your weight equally on all four corners of both feet.
3. Begin to shift the weight over to the right foot, lifting the left foot off the floor.
4. Bend the left knee, bringing the sole of the left foot high onto the inner right thigh.
5. Press the foot into the thigh and the thigh back into the foot.
6. Try not to let the right hip jut out. Keep both hips squared towards the front.
7. Focus on something that doesn't move to help you keep your balance.
8. Repeat while standing on the left foot.

■ Outdoor yoga

Downward Facing Dog

1. Come to your hands and knees with the wrists underneath the shoulders and the knees underneath the hips.
2. Curl the toes under and push back raising the hips while straightening the legs.
3. Spread the fingers and ground down from the forearms into the fingertips.
4. Outwardly rotate the upper arms broadening the collarbones.
5. Let the head hang, move the shoulder blades away from the ears towards the hips.
6. Engage the quadriceps strongly to take the weight off the arms, making this a resting pose.
7. Rotate the thighs inward, keep the tail high and sink your heels to the floor.
8. Check that the distance between your hands and feet is correct by coming forward to a plank position. The distance between the hands and feet should be the same in these two poses. Do not step the feet toward the hands in Down Dog in order the get the heels to the floor. This will happen eventually as the muscles lengthen.

■ Outdoor yoga

Crow pose

1. Bending the knees slightly, bring your palms flat on the floor about shoulder's distance apart.
2. Place the knees on the back of the upper arms.
3. Start to come forward, lifting the head as you go.
4. Take one foot and then the other off the floor so you come to balance with both feet up.

■ Outdoor yoga

Fish Pose

1. Come to lie on the back.
2. Come up onto the elbows.
3. Slide the body towards the back of the mat while keeping the forearms in place and puffing up the chest.
4. Drop the crown of the head back to the floor, opening the throat.
5. To come out, press strongly into the forearms and raise the head off the floor.
6. Release the upper body to the floor.

■ 14 days of training by running in the park

FIRST WEEK

Monday:
Free

Tuesday:
35 minutes of tempo training

Wednesday:
Free

Thursday:
50 minutes of stamina training

Friday:
Free

Saturday:
40 minutes of "fartlek"

Sunday:
30 minutes of recovery

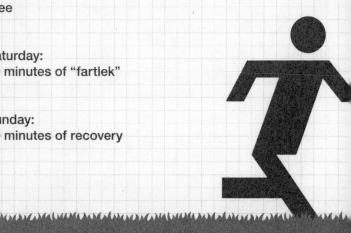

◼ 14 days of training by running in the park

SECOND WEEK

Monday:
Free

Tuesday:
40 minutes of tempo training

Wednesday:
Free

Thursday:
60 minutes of stamina training

Friday:
Free

Saturday:
40 minutes of "fartlek"

Sunday:
30 minutes of recovery

■ Training journal

Date:

Exercise:

Repetitions:

Date:

Exercise:

Repetitions:

Date:

Exercise:

Repetitions:

■ Training journal

Date:

Exercise:

Repetitions:

Date:

Exercise:

Repetitions:

Date:

Exercise:

Repetitions:

■ Training journal

Date:

Exercise:

Repetitions:

Date:

Exercise:

Repetitions:

Date:

Exercise:

Repetitions:

■ Training journal

Date:

Exercise:

Repetitions:

Date:

Exercise:

Repetitions:

Date:

Exercise:

Repetitions:

■ Training journal

Date:

Exercise:

Repetitions:

Date:

Exercise:

Repetitions:

Date:

Exercise:

Repetitions:

■ Training journal

Date:

Exercise:

Repetitions:

Date:

Exercise:

Repetitions:

Date:

Exercise:

Repetitions:

■ Pep talk for training!

Decide what days to exercise and make room for it in your calendar straight away. This way, other obligations won't get in the way!

If the exercises are too hard, reduce the number of repetitions. Remember to do the exercises in an even pace.

Flirt during running! That guarantees a more fun training!

Wildlife

■ Birdwatching - How to

The park can be an excellent place to observe birds. Here's a guide for doing so!

1. Use your ears to detect where the birds are.

2. Follow the sound with your eyes.

3. Walk quietly up to where the bird song or sound is coming from. Don't get too close or the bird will fly away.

5. Use a pair of binoculars to get a good look at the bird!

■ Urban wild life

You don't have to be in a forest to see wild animals, it's enough just going to the park. Here's some info about some of the most common ones.

Badger
With their striking facial markings, badgers are easily recognizable. But to actually see a badger is quite hard because the badger only ventures out at night. If you do want to however, the best time to look for badgers is between April and May.

Raccoon
The raccoon is sometimes referred to as "masked bandits" and they're easily recognizable. They are excellent climbers – look up in the trees! You are most likely to see them at night time.

Skunk
The skunk doesn't need a visual presentation. The horrible smell makes it easy to detect the skunk!

Bat
Look up! The bat flies in forests and climb trees.

Remember! Don't feed the animals!

■ Fishing guide

Many parks allow fishing. Here's how you do it.

Step one: catch the fish

1) Choose a good location.

2) Get a fishingrod, a hook and a bait
(like corn kernels or bread dough).

3) Catch the line and wait!

Step two: kill the fish

1) Do a quick jerk backward and up.
2) Grab hold of the fish.
3) Remove the hook.
4) Kill the fish.
5) You can also let the fish go and collect

alot of **good karma.**

■ Squirrel Facts

Squirrel's belong to the order "Rodentia", with 1650 species and it is the largest group of living mammals. It also comprises forty percent of all present day mammal species.

There are over 365 species of squirrels in seven families. They include the tree squirrel, ground squirrel, and flying squirrel. Plus many squirrel-like mammals such as the gopher, ground hog and prairie dog.

Squirrels are the most active in late winter, when the mating season begins. The males will chase a females, as well as chase off other suitors. This ritual of chasing occurs through the trees at top speed, while they perform some of the most breathtaking acrobatics imaginable.

Squirrels are usually born in the early spring. A baby squirrel weighs approximately one ounce at birth and is about one inch long. They do not have hair or teeth, and are virtually blind for the first six to eight weeks.

In the summer squirrels are most active two to three hours after sunrise, then they'll rest in the afternoon. Resuming activity again two hours before sunset. The squirrel will retire to its nest well before dark. In the winter, the squirrel will complete its activities between dawn and mid-day, and will remain in or around the nest until the next day. During winter storms, or severe cold, the squirrel may not leave the nest for days.

■ Squirrel Facts

An adult squirrel normally lives alone. But will, in severe cold, share its nest with other squirrels to conserve body heat. But once the temperature rises, the guests will be on their way!

Squirrels eyes are located high, and on each side of their head. This allows them a wide field of vision, without turning their head, which is great if you are constantly on the lookout for enemies. Or if you have many television sets.

The gray squirrels diet consists of nuts, seeds and fruit. But it will eat bird eggs, bugs, and even an animal carcass if there is no other food source available. The gray squirrel requires some salt in its diet, and may find this salt in the soil along roads where snow and ice may have been. The average adult squirrel needs to eat about a pound of food a week to maintain an active life.

Squirrels chew on tree branches to sharpen and clean their teeth. That's why you may see many small branches on the ground around large trees. They will also chew on power lines for the same reason, something that has caused many major power outages, and squirrel deaths. It might be explained by the size of squirrel's brain – the size of a walnut.

■ Squirrel Facts

Squirrels communicate through a series of chirps. The frequency, and the duration of the notes communicate everything from laughter to alarm. Their frequency range is normally between .01 KHz. and 10 KHz. (kilohertz). These sounds when used in conjunction with tail gestures, form the basis for squirrel communication.

A squirrel will break the shell of a nut with its teeth, then clean the nut by licking it or rubbing it on its face before it is buried. This action applies a scent to the nut which helps the squirrel find it later, even under a foot of snow.

Don't try this at home

The squirrel's erratic path while crossing a street is an attempt to confuse the oncoming vehicle, thereby causing it to change direction. This is obliviously the squirrels biggest, and often last mistake.

■ Squirrel Facts

The male tree squirrel takes twice as long, as the female, to groom itself. They are in fact the cleanest animal in the rodent family.

A squirrels teeth grow continuously. Their incisor's will grow six inches per year, but stay short due to the constant wear they receive.

...or this...

The most common type of squirrel bite is a result of feeding a squirrel by hand. Never hold the food between your fingers, chances are very good you will be bitten. A squirrel's eyes are always looking for predators and they rarely focus on what they are eating.

■ Insect facts

Did you know that there are many more kinds of insects on earth than any other kind of living creature? It's hard to imagine, but 95% of all the animal species on earth are insects! Millions of insects can exist in a single acre of land! Over one million species have been discovered by scientists, and they think that there might be ten times that many that haven't been named yet! In fact, one out of every four animals on earth is a beetle. Scientists estimate that 10% of the animal biomass of the world is ants, and another 10% is termites. This means that ants and termites make up an incredible 20% of the total animal biomass of this planet!

Insects eat more plants than all other creatures on earth together. They are also so important in the breakdown of plant and animal matter, that without them, we would have a world covered with dead plants and animals! In addition to all of this, insects are a major food source for many other animals.

Insects are incredibly adaptable creatures and have evolved to live successfully in most environments on earth, including deserts and even the Antarctic. The only place where insects are not commonly found is in the oceans. Insects have an amazing number of differences in size, shape, and behavior, but they all have 4 characteristics in common.

■ Insect facts

- three body parts - a head, thorax, and abdomen
- six jointed legs
- two antennae to sense the world around them
- an exoskeleton (outside skeleton)

Insects are directly useful to humans by producing honey, silk, wax, and other products. They are also important as pollinators of crops, natural enemies of pests, scavengers, and food for other creatures. Insects are often considered major pests of humans and domesticated animals because they destroy crops and carry diseases, but actually, less than one percent of insect species are pests, and only a few hundred of these are consistently a problem.

■ Wildlife journal

- animals I've seen in the park

Date:

Park:

Animal:

Date:

Park:

Animal:

Date:

Park:

Animal:

■ Wildlife journal

- animals I've seen in the park

Date:

Park:

Animal:

Date:

Park:

Animal:

Date:

Park:

Animal:

■ Wildlife journal

- animals I've seen in the park

Date:

Park:

Animal:

Date:

Park:

Animal:

Date:

Park:

Animal:

■ Wildlife journal

- animals I've seen in the park

Date:

Park:

Animal:

Date:

Park:

Animal:

Date:

Park:

Animal:

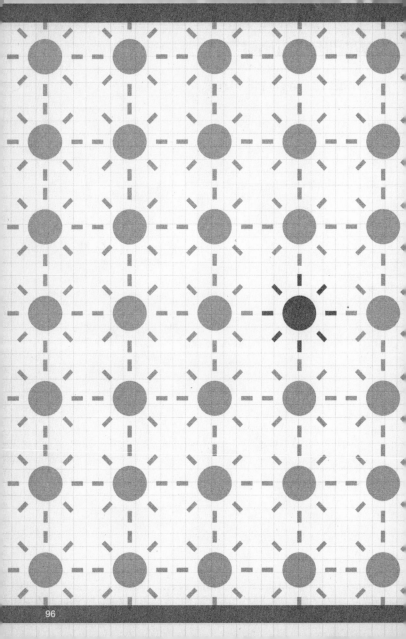

Park trivia

■ Trivia

- Central Park is almost twice as large as Monaco and nearly eight times as large as the Vatican City.

- Birkenhead Park in Birkenhead, Merseyside, is commonly regarded as the first civic public park in the world. Birkenhead Park opened on 5 April 1847.

- There are 8,968 benches in Central park.

- The famous Speaker's Corner is located in Hyde Park.

- The fountain featured in the opening credits of Married With Children is the Buckingham Fountain and it is located in Grant Park in Chicago.

- The largest city park in the U.S. is South Mountain Park in Phoenix, Arizona, which comprises 16,169 acres.

■ Trivia

- The largest city park in Europe is Phoenix Park in Dublin, Ireland, which comprises 1,800 acres.

- Ueno Park is Tokyo's first public park and was opened in 1873. Ueno Park is today one of Tokyo's biggest tourist attractions.

- The park bench used in the film Notting Hill now 'lives' in Queens Gardens in East Perth, Western Australia.

 - Central park is visitied by 25 million people every year. Central Park is the park most featured in films. It's been in more than 240 feature films since 1908.

■ Facts about some great parks

Central Park is a large public, urban park (843 acres, 3.41 km², 1.32 mi²; a rectangle 2.6 statute miles by 0.5 statute mile, or 4.1 km × 830 m) in the borough of Manhattan in New York City. With about twenty-five million visitors annually, Central Park is the most visited city park in the United States and its appearance in many movies and television shows has made it famous.

The park was designed by landscape designer Frederick Law Olmsted and architect Calvert Vaux, who went on to collaborate on Brooklyn's Prospect Park. Central Park has been a National Historic Landmark since 1963.

Central Park is larger than two of the world's smallest nations. It is almost twice as large as Monaco and nearly eight times as large as Vatican City.

Legendary entertainer Diana Ross has a playground named after her in Central Park, the Diana Ross Playground.

■ Facts about some great parks

On Saturday, February 8, 1964, as part of the Beatles' first visit to America, John Lennon, Paul McCartney and Ringo Starr visited Central Park while entertaining photographers and members of the press. George Harrison stayed back at the group's suite at the Plaza Hotel, due to a bout with tonsillitis. On Lennon's birthday, October 9, 1985, Yoko Ono helped inaugurate the Strawberry Fields memorial, created as a tribute to him following his murder on December 8, 1980.

Sheep actually grazed on the Sheep Meadow from the 1860s until 1934, when they were moved upstate since it was feared they would be used for food by impoverished depression-era New Yorkers.

Fairmount Park in Philadelphia is actually more than 5 times as large as Central Park. Despite this, Central Park has 2.5 times as many visitors.

The real-estate value of Central Park is estimated to be $528,783,552,000 according to the property-appraisal firm Miller Samuel.

■ Facts about some great parks

Charles Ives wrote a piece called 'Central Park in the Dark'. Tunes of the day are included, such as 'Hello, My Baby', and music to represent a passing fire engine and a horse going through the fence.

Birkenhead Park on the Wirral, Merseyside, UK, is twinned with Central Park

Central Park constitutes its own United States census tract, number 143. According to Census 2000, the park's population is eighteen persons, twelve male and six fe-male, with a median age of 38.5 years, and a household size of 2.33, over 3 households.

■ Facts about some great parks

Golden Gate Park, located in San Francisco, California, is a large urban park consisting of 1017 acres (4.1 km^2, 1.6 mi^2) of public grounds. Configured as a rectangle, it is similar in shape but 174 acres (0.7 km^2, 0.27 mi^2) larger than Central Park in New York, to which it is often compared. With 13 million visitors annually, Golden Gate is the third most visited city park in America (after Central Park and Lincoln Park in Chicago).

There are a number of naturalistically landscaped lakes throughout the park, several linked together into chains, with pumped water creating flowing creeks.

Did-you-know!

A notable bronze statue of Don Quixote and his companion, Sancho Panza may be found in one of the many walks in the park.

A paddock corrals a small herd of bison, captive in the Park since 1892.

■ Facts about some great parks

Lincoln Park is a 1,200 acre (4.9 km², 1.875 mi²) park along Chicago, Illinois' lakefront facing Lake Michigan.

The park stretches from North Avenue (1600 N) on the south to Ardmore (5900 N), just north of the Lake Shore Drive terminus at North Hollywood Avenue.

It is Chicago's largest public park. It has many recreational facilities including 15 baseball areas, 6 basketball courts, 2 softball courts, 35 tennis courts, 163 volley ball courts, field houses, a golf course, and a popular fitness center.

It includes a number of harbours with boating facilities, as well as public beaches. There are landscaped gardens, a zoo, the Lincoln Park Conservatory, the Peggy Notebaert Nature Museum, and a theater on the lake with regular outdoor performances during the summer.

Added to the National Register of Historic Places in 1994, Lincoln Park began its existence as City Cemetery.

■ Facts about some great parks

Griffith Park is a large public park at the eastern end of the Santa Monica Mountains. It is situated in the Los Feliz neighborhood of Los Angeles, California. The park covers 4,210 acres (17 km²) of land, making it one of the largest urban parks in North America. It is the second-largest city park in California, after Mission Trails Preserve in San Diego. It has also been referred to as the Central Park of Los Angeles.

After successfully investing in mining, Colonel Griffith J. Griffith purchased Rancho Los Feliz (near the Los Angeles River) in 1882 and created an ostrich farm there. Although ostrich feathers were commonly used in making women's hats in the late-1800s, Col. Griffith created the farm primarily to lure residents of Los Angeles to his nearby property developments. After the property rush peaked, and supposedly spooked by the ghost of Antonio Feliz (a previous owner of the property) he donated 3015 acres (12 km²) to the city of Los Angeles on December 16, 1896.

■ Facts about some great parks

Afterward Griffith was tried and convicted for shooting and severely wounding his wife. When released from prison, he attempted to fund the construction of an observatory, planetarium, and amphitheater in the park. However, his reputation in the city was tainted by his crime, so the city refused his money.

In 1912, Griffith designated 100 acres (400,000 m²) of the park, at its northwest corner along the Los Angeles River, be used to "do something to further aviation." The Griffith Park Aerodrome was the result. Aviation pioneers such as Glenn L. Martin and Silas Christoffersen used it. The aerodrome then passed to the National Guard Air Service. Air operations continued on a 2,000-foot (600 m)-long runway (610 m) until 1939, when the City Planning commission complained that a military airport violated the terms of Griffith's deed.

Sitting atop the southern slope of Mount Hollywood in Griffith Park, the Griffith Observatory is featured in the classic film, Rebel Without A Cause (1955) starring: James Dean, Natalie Wood, and Sal Mineo, and serves as the backdrop for key scenes that are threaded throughout the movie. Moreover, the steps of the Observatory set the stage for the film's climactic ending. Notably, James Dean, who played the lead role of Jim Stark in the movie, also shot a Coca-Cola commercial in Griffith Park during his early years as an actor. A bronze bust of him is on the grounds just outside the Observatory's domed building

■ Facts about some great parks

Hyde Park is one of the largest parks in central London, England and one of the Royal Parks of London, famous for its Speakers' Corner. The park is divided in two by the Serpentine Lake.

The park is contiguous with Kensington Gardens, which is widely assumed to be part of Hyde Park, but is technically separate. Hyde Park is 350 acres (140 hectare/1.4 km²) and Kensington Gardens is 275 acres (110 ha/1.1 km²) giving an overall area of 625 acres (250 ha/2.5 km²).

One of the most important events to take place in the park was the Great Exhibition of 1851, for which the Crystal Palace was constructed on the south side of the park. The public in general did not want the building to remain in the park after the conclusion of the exhibition, and the design architect, Joseph Paxton, raised funds and purchased it. He had it moved to Sydenham Hill in South London

■ Facts about some great parks

Kensington Gardens, once the private gardens of Kensington Palace, is one of the Royal Parks of London, lying immediately to the west of Hyde Park. Most of it is in the City of Westminster, but a small section to the west is in the Royal Borough of Kensington and Chelsea. It covers 275 acres (1.1 km²).

The park is famous to generations of British schoolchildren as the setting of J.M. Barrie's book Peter Pan in Kensington Gardens, a prelude to the character's famous adventures in Neverland. The fairies of the gardens are first described in Thomas Tickell's 1722 poem Kensington Gardens. Both the book and the character are honored with the iconic Peter Pan statue located in the park.

St James's Park is the oldest of the Royal Parks of London. It is situated in the City of Westminster, London, just east of Buckingham Palace and west of Whitehall and Downing Street. The St James's area, including St. James's Palace, is just to the north. The park is 23 hectares (58 acres) in size.

On James I's accession to the throne in 1603, he ordered the park drained and landscaped and kept various exotic animals in the park, including camels, crocodiles and an elephant, as well as aviaries of exotic birds along the south.

■ Facts about some great parks

Regent's Park (officially The Regent's Park) is often described as the greatest of the London's parks with its perfect combination of architecture, landscape and surrounding urban fabric. Covering 166 hectares, the park was designed in 1811 by architect John Nash.

Originally a royal hunting ground and farmland, it became an urban park when the Prince Regent commissioned John Nash to come up with a grand design. The Prince wanted a grand vista and a processional way from his home, Carlton House, to a regal park.

The vision was to create a park resembling a country estate with grand houses on its outer edges, villas in the centre and park villages nearby.
Today the park is as popular as ever with a new generation of Londoners.

■ Park notes - Things to do

■ Park notes - Weird dreams

Park notes - Don't forget list

■ Park notes - Business ideas

■ Park notes - My life in 1 year

■ Park notes - My life in 5 years

◼ Park notes - Great pet names

■ Park notes - Places I'm traveling to

■ Park notes - Books I plan to read

■ Park notes - Movies I plan to watch

■ Park notes - A list of great gifts

■ Park notes - Things I like about myself

■ Park notes - What to do with a million

■ Park notes - How to make a million

■ Park notes - Candy toplist

■ Park notes - Food toplist

■ Park notes - Superpowers I wish I had

■ Park notes - Best songs in the world

■ Park notes - Favorite names

■ Park notes - Things I like starting on F

■ Great park books!

Pride and Prejudice, Jane Austen

His Dark Materials, Philip Pullman

The Hitchhiker's Guide to the Galaxy, Douglas Adams

To Kill a Mockingbird, Harper Lee

Winnie the Pooh, AA Milne

Nineteen Eighty-Four, George Orwell

The Lion, the Witch and the Wardrobe, CS Lewis

Jane Eyre, Charlotte Brontë

Catch-22, Joseph Heller

Wuthering Heights, Emily Brontë

Birdsong, Sebastian Faulks

Rebecca, Daphne du Maurier

The Catcher in the Rye, JD Salinger

The Wind in the Willows, Kenneth Grahame

Great Expectations, Charles Dickens

Little Women, Louisa May Alcott

Captain Corelli's Mandolin, Louis de Bernieres

War and Peace, Leo Tolstoy

Gone with the Wind, Margaret Mitchell

Tess Of The D'Urbervilles, Thomas Hardy

Middlemarch, George Eliot

A Prayer For Owen Meany, John Irving

The Grapes Of Wrath, John Steinbeck

Alice's Adventures In Wonderland, Lewis Carroll

The Story Of Tracy Beaker, Jacqueline Wilson

One Hundred Years Of Solitude, Gabriel García Márquez

The Pillars Of The Earth, Ken Follett

■ Great park books!

David Copperfield, Charles Dickens

Charlie And The Chocolate Factory, Roald Dahl

Treasure Island, Robert Louis Stevenson

A Town Like Alice, Nevil Shute

Persuasion, Jane Austen

Dune, Frank Herbert

Emma, Jane Austen

Anne Of Green Gables, LM Montgomery

Watership Down, Richard Adams

The Great Gatsby, F Scott Fitzgerald

The Count Of Monte Cristo, Alexandre Dumas

Brideshead Revisited, Evelyn Waugh

Animal Farm, George Orwell

Far From The Madding Crowd, Thomas Hardy

Goodnight Mister Tom, Michelle Magorian

The Shell Seekers, Rosamunde Pilcher

The Secret Garden, Frances Hodgson Burnett

Of Mice And Men, John Steinbeck

The Stand, Stephen King

Anna Karenina, Leo Tolstoy

A Suitable Boy, Vikram Seth

The BFG, Roald Dahl

Swallows And Amazons, Arthur Ransome

Black Beauty, Anna Sewell

Artemis Fowl, Eoin Colfer

Crime And Punishment, Fyodor Dostoyevsky

Noughts And Crosses, Malorie Blackman

■ Great park books!

Memoirs Of A Geisha, Arthur Golden

A Tale Of Two Cities, Charles Dickens

The Thorn Birds, Colleen McCollough

Mort, Terry Pratchett

The Magic Faraway Tree, Enid Blyton

The Magus, John Fowles

Good Omens, Terry Pratchett and Neil Gaiman

Guards! Guards!, Terry Pratchett

Lord Of The Flies, William Golding

Perfume, Patrick Süskind

The Ragged Trousered Philanthropists, Robert Tressell

Night Watch, Terry Pratchett

Bridget Jones's Diary, Helen Fielding

The Secret History, Donna Tartt

The Woman In White, Wilkie Collins

Ulysses, James Joyce

Bleak House, Charles Dickens

Double Act, Jacqueline Wilson

I Capture The Castle, Dodie Smith

Holes, Louis Sachar

Gormenghast, Mervyn Peake

The God Of Small Things, Arundhati Roy

Vicky Angel, Jacqueline Wilson

Brave New World, Aldous Huxley

Cold Comfort Farm, Stella Gibbons

Magician, Raymond E Feist

On The Road, Jack Kerouac

■ Great park books!

The Godfather, Mario Puzo

The Clan Of The Cave Bear, Jean M Auel

The Colour Of Magic, Terry Pratchett

The Alchemist, Paulo Coelho

Katherine, Anya Seton

Kane And Abel, Jeffrey Archer

Love In The Time Of Cholera, Gabriel García Márquez

Girls In Love, Jacqueline Wilson

The Princess Diaries, Meg Cabot

Midnight's Children, Salman Rushdie

■ 10 reasons why parks are great

1. They are a city's lungs.

2. They provide shade in the summer.

3. They are great for exercising.

4. They are fun to hang out in.

5. They are home to the notorious and pearshaped Parkpeople (not many have seen them).

6. Squirrels like parks. Squirrels are fuzzy. We like fuzzy things. So we like parks.

7. PARK. Now take the P away. You get ARK. Now add NOAH'S. See the connection?

8. If you have a dog and don't want it to poop in your living room, the park is usually a good alternative.

9. Everyone likes the color green.

10. We can think of only 9 reasons why parks are great so this last one is kind of a stretch.

■ Park diary - favorite park

Name of the park:

The first time I visited this park:

The last time I visited this park:

My best memory from this park:

My favorite spot in this park:

The weirdest thing I've seen in this park:

This is what I enjoy doing in this park:

■ Park diary - favorite park

Name of park:

The first time I visited this park:

The last time I visited this park:

My best memory from this park:

My favorite spot in this park:

The weirdest thing I've seen in this park:

This is what I enjoy doing in this park:

■ Park diary - favorite park

Name of park:

The first time I visited this park:

The last time I visited this park:

My best memory from this park:

My favorite spot in this park:

The weirdest thing I've seen in this park:

This is what I enjoy doing in this park:

◼ Do's and Don't's

Feeding of birds and other wildlife is prohibited

Don't park on the handicap parking spots

Don't barbeque under trees

Don't leave litter in the park

Don't break any branches

Keep your dog in a leash where it's claimed

Don't ride your bicycle where it's not okay

Be considerate to others

■ Do's and Don't's

Do not walk in planting beds

Removal of any City property is prohibited

Reduce radio volume near residential buildings, or if other visitors request it

Horseback riding prohibited except in designated areas

Dogs and/or domestic animals must be kept on a leash

Dogs are not allowed in playgrounds

Keep all vehicles on roadways

Park in designated areas only

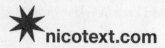
nicotext.com